This book is dedicated to my
Lil' "O" and my Lil' "A".
May God bless you both with
imagination and creativity.
And, may your life's journey
bring about many stories of your own...

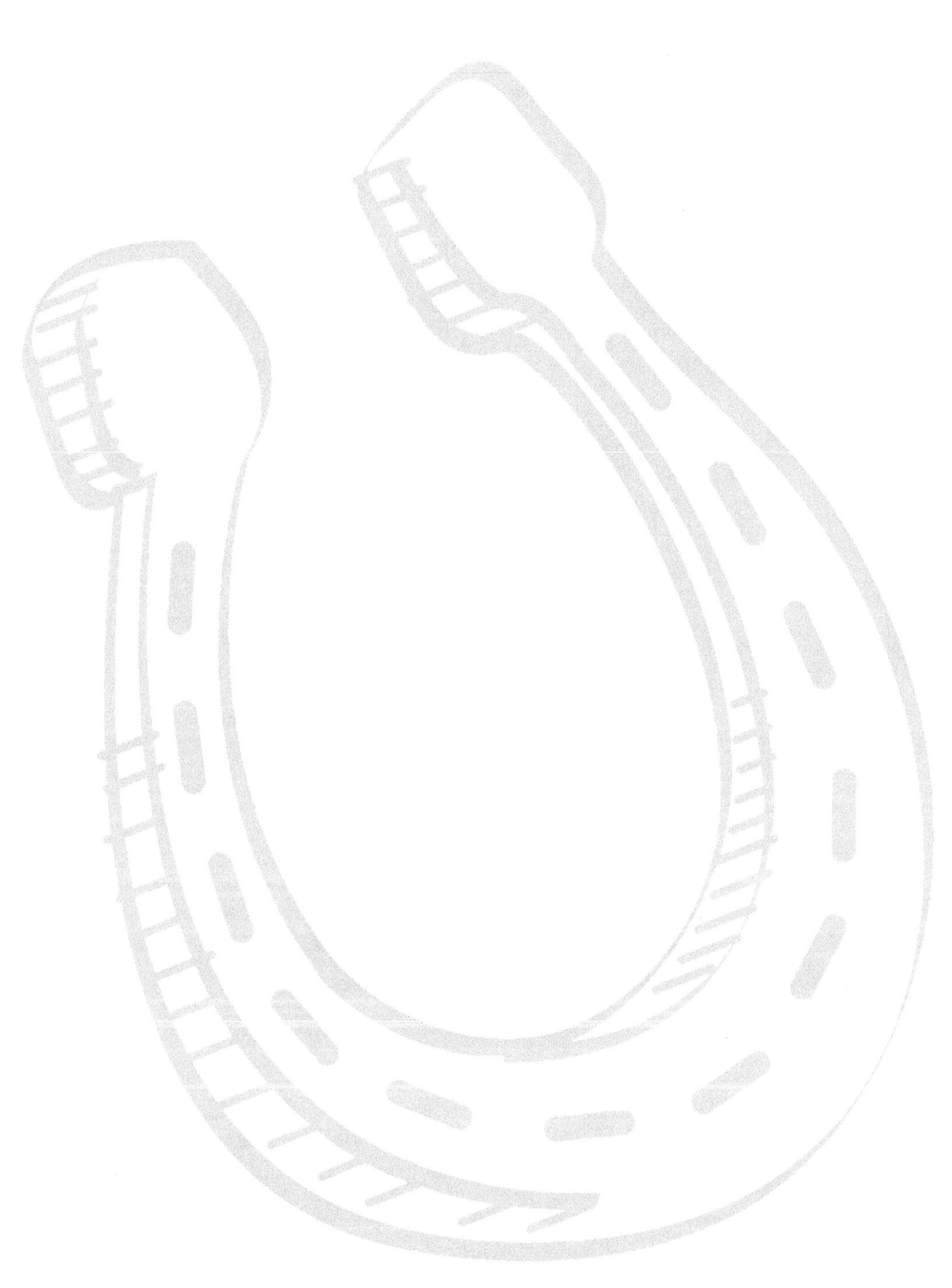

If you are going to be a traveler there are a few things to consider. Wherever you are going, you have to enjoy getting there. Take the road less traveled. Bring a book with no writing on the pages, and fill it with your own words...

Once upon a time a journey began. Like every journey, things happen along the way. As the years go on, tales and lore are collected. Shells and fossils, arrowheads and old horseshoes... Whatever the collection, it tells a story. The twisting and turning together with the events of long ago until now. You combine the collected treasures with all the events and a colorful yarn unravels, with many twists and secrets told...

It happened in the old of New England. Deep in the woods of the trodden upon ground that our forefathers fought the revolutionary war upon. It is there that Aunt Edie had her inn. Built in the 1700's, everyone you talked to said that George Washington himself stayed there. He rode the same white horse that he is sitting on by the Potomac. In fact, that very horse stayed in the barn by the inn...So they say. The inn was 4 stories. That means four floors, plus an attic and a cellar. So, I guess six altogether. Each room and floor had a name, and a story. One room, for example, is called The Green Room. Deep and mysterious is the lore of The Green Room. Tales abound of George's brigade meeting secretly there to form the night attacks on the red coats. There was a large fire place coated with many layers of soot. In the evening the room had a soft, dim glow. The dark green walls flickered as the embers from the fire danced across. Tobacco filled pipes with gray strings of smoke floated up; you could hear their hushed murmurings of war strategies.

My Aunt Edie took great pride in her inn. Breakfast was served with giant blueberry muffins made with wild blueberries picked from the mountain top, small and sweet. Hot coffee gurgled in the percolator, and condensation beaded up on the pipes of the indoor water pump from the cold deep water well. The rooms had low ceilings, and wide plank floors with deep grooves from the hooves of horses. Now, I could go on forever about the way the inn smelled. When a place is that old, it has a mixture of fragrances. Every meal cooked, every bouquet of wild flowers, all the fragrances of every season for hundreds of years made its way into the grains of those old paneled walls. There was the mixed aroma of fine boot leather, roasted beef, aged pine wood and wild mint hanging for tea. And, of course the undeniable smell of horses! If one was going to describe the smell of a horse you could say it is a combination of strength, saddle leather, perspiration (which isn't bad), but sort of like a farm in the woodland. Like rich soil just waiting to have a seed imbedded into it.

When you turn off the main road to go to the inn, the way narrows. It is one of those "not-so-traveled-roads" where the grass grows in the center. Maples with their wide, hundred-year-old trunks, line each side of the path. Their branches, thick overhead, crisscross the road creating mosaic patterns of light and shadows. You feel sort of regal as you move underneath, as though they were guards, crossing their swords above. The inn is a big white farm house. There really isn't anything remarkable about the way it looks. A large deep porch wraps around it with thick wood slats, heavy with many years of paint.   There is a large barn across from it, gray and weather worn. It has a loft where sacks of grain are stored for Aunt Edie's horses, Nelson and Blueskin. The barn has a pathway that cuts across the road and yard, from its side door to the back door of the kitchen. It has elaborate carvings, made by the soldiers that stayed at the inn; beautiful expressions for their wives and loved ones, who await their safe return home. There are stalls in the barn for the horses, but most of the time they are in the yard of the inn, eating the clover and drinking the rain water collected in the barrel. They stay in the barn most nights...

As you lay in the feather bed with the iron railings, the aroma from the muffins would waft up all the way to the fourth floor from the kitchen. In the summer cool breezes would blow in the open window from nearby Mount Wachusett. Wild roses and violet fragrances came with it...You never forget this journey. Like the rich carvings in the deep planks of the barn, they are etched in my memory.

In this part of the world the seasons of change are very important. You always stock up on food and supplies for those long, cold and bleak months of winter. In August you can have a sunny warm day, but then the next day may bring frost or icy rain. The horses were not especially fond of the cold weather. If it was time for a ride and the weather was bad, they would hide. "Horses don't hide!", that is what you're thinking right now, but they were not to be found. If they did come around, they would tighten their lips to keep you from putting in the bit.

When Aunt Edie called them from the back porch, off the kitchen, "Nelson! Blueskin!", they would come, knowing it was time. Some say horses are dumb. Be careful to never let your horse hear you say such a thing. They show their cleverness in different ways, such as their body language or how they respond to your friendship. You can let them know that you care by giving them jelly beans, carrots, apples, and sweet green grasses, like the ones that grow by the pond.

Horses like to hang out...with other horses. They become good friends with each other. As for the riding thing—they can take it or leave it. Sometimes they would rather just walk with you instead of under you. They sort of have their own ideas about things. They won't curl up by your feet like a dog, but they will follow you around like one, and can be very playful.

When I was young, our neighbors had a pony named, Prince. He would "hang out" in their kitchen in the morning sometimes. My friend would ride him to my house to get me. Then we would ride him back to hers. Many times he would take us through the giant lilac bush, trying to knock us off his back. Then he would gladly walk alongside us for the rest of the way home. A hundred years ago a horse was like your car, that's how you got around. So, having a good relationship with your horse was especially important back then.

Taking care of that old inn was a handful for my aunt. Going up and down those stairs really took its toll.   When all of her help had gone home for the day, the old farm house, with its creaking wood and slight whistle from the wind was all to be heard. She would sit in The Green Room, staring into the flames of the fire place, with her roast beef sandwich and hot tea. Blueskin and Nelson would remind her that they were near.   Blueskin especially was fond of Edie. He would nuzzle her softly on the head with his warm nose, while making soft humming noises. Nelson stood by closely, propping his back foot forward; ready to close his eyes for the night. Aunt Edie closed her eyes too, and heard the soft voices of the men telling their stories of war and stretching their tales from long ago. As she made her way upstairs she reminded Blueskin and Nelson that, "Tomorrow is a special day because my favorite niece will be coming for a visit. Be prepared, our guest will be arriving early."

There is nothing at all like a visit to the old inn. There is a certain reverence about the place. The ground on which it is built is sacred; Men died on these grounds. In the days before our country and constitution were established, they rode into battle to preserve what they and their families had left their homes in Europe for... Freedom!

In those days traveling in the winter weather could be harsh. They could find themselves traveling in cold winds, snow, or freezing rain. The men could almost always expect a warm meal and clean bed at the inn. Thin biscuits with slices of cold beef, accompanied by wine in warmed pewter mugs (made from the pear trees that grew down by the pond) would be waiting in their rooms. Fires were lit in the rooms, causing a soft orange light to spill out from the windows onto the snow covered grounds, enveloping the farmhouse in a soft glow. Secret messengers had trails through the woods. They would come ahead on foot to announce to the innkeepers of the arrival of soldiers, many of whom might be injured and in need of medicine.

The innkeeper would light a special lamp to tell the soldiers that the inn was safe. Those lamps had a horseshoe etched in the glass. This was the code that marked the inns that were part of the secret underground. Only a select few knew about it. The arriving soldiers would give the sign of the horse shoe, indicating to the keeper that they were not British soldiers, but Revolutionaries. They would arrive at the inn worn out and hungry. Their horses needed special care, to ensure they would be fresh and ready to move out at dawn. They would bathe the horses in large tubs with warm water and put blankets over them. A mixture of brown sugar, oats, molasses, carrots, apples and hay would be laid out for them to eat.

It was said that George and his horse, were so close that he would follow him to his room on the fourth floor. He loved the Inn at the foot of Mt. Wachusett. It was deep into the country, and far off the main roadway. It was a hidden place where he knew it was safe to rendezvous with his men. The Inn would always have a lantern burning to help them find their way. Even if it was late into the night, the innkeeper would always be prepared for the weary travelers. The secret codes assured them that the place was clear of anything suspicious. It wasn't until many years after the war ended that these inns were discovered to have been the military meeting places such as they were.

As I open the car door it hits me... That sweet air blowing down from ole Wachusett brings all the fragrances from those enchanting woods with it. It is close to evening, that moment that is referred to as "dusk" (the soft twilight, between day and night). Everything has sort of a golden hew. Blueskin and Nelson remember us, or, the jelly beans I always have for them! I guess I relate to horses in that way... they have a sweet tooth, and so do I! They follow us into the small kitchen area where Aunt Edie is preparing lentils and beef. The evenings are starting to be a little chilly so she thought a hearty stew was in order. Pulling the last of the butter lettuce and snow peas from the garden, she tossed a salad with some sweet apple dressing.

After dinner we sat in the green room. Hard maple burned bright in the fireplace. We sat for a while and enjoyed the quiet. The windows, slightly opened, allowed us to hear that clear, pensive song from a hermit thrush... "Too teedle-teedle-teedle." We talked about our travels, and our early departure in the morning. The enchantment of The Green Room took me back. I, too, heard the murmurings of the soldiers. Their mud-caked riding boots and muskets piled and stacked by the door, I could sense the earthy aroma of gun powder and wet earth. Aunt Edie spoke and brought me back to the present. We made our ascent to the special suite, with a bathroom, on the fourth floor. "I know how long those four flights can be when you're waking up in the morning. It is a long haul! Blueskin and Nelson will be there in your room waiting for you when you get up. They will give you a ride down to breakfast."   This is one of my favorite traditions. Waking up to see Blueskin and Nelson in my room, I would remember the stories that were told...

George would wake up and scrape the ice off the inside of the windows. The fresh snowfall from overnight would cover any foot prints made the day before, concealing their presence at the inn. This gave the revolutionary soldiers an extra advantage, should the enemy be near. Mentally preparing himself for the long journey ahead, George pulled up his wool stockings and undergarments, rubbing out the cold stiffness as he did so. He then buttoned his shirt, fastened his breeches and mounted Blueskin. George would crouch low resting his head on Blueskin's neck, so he wouldn't bump his head on the low ceiling beams.

You might ask why the horses stayed in the rooms... "A preposterous legend," you might say! Sometimes things don't have to be explained. Maybe it was just that George and his beloved horses were that close. They rode together every day. He cared for them every moment. They had an in depth dependency upon each other. George could have never been successful in battle if it were not for his horse companions. So, when I sat on the back of Nelson or Blueskin, and made our way down to breakfast, you could plainly see it wasn't unusual for them...nor difficult. They scaled the four flights with effortless ease and agility. It was as if they had been doing it for hundreds of years...

THE
END

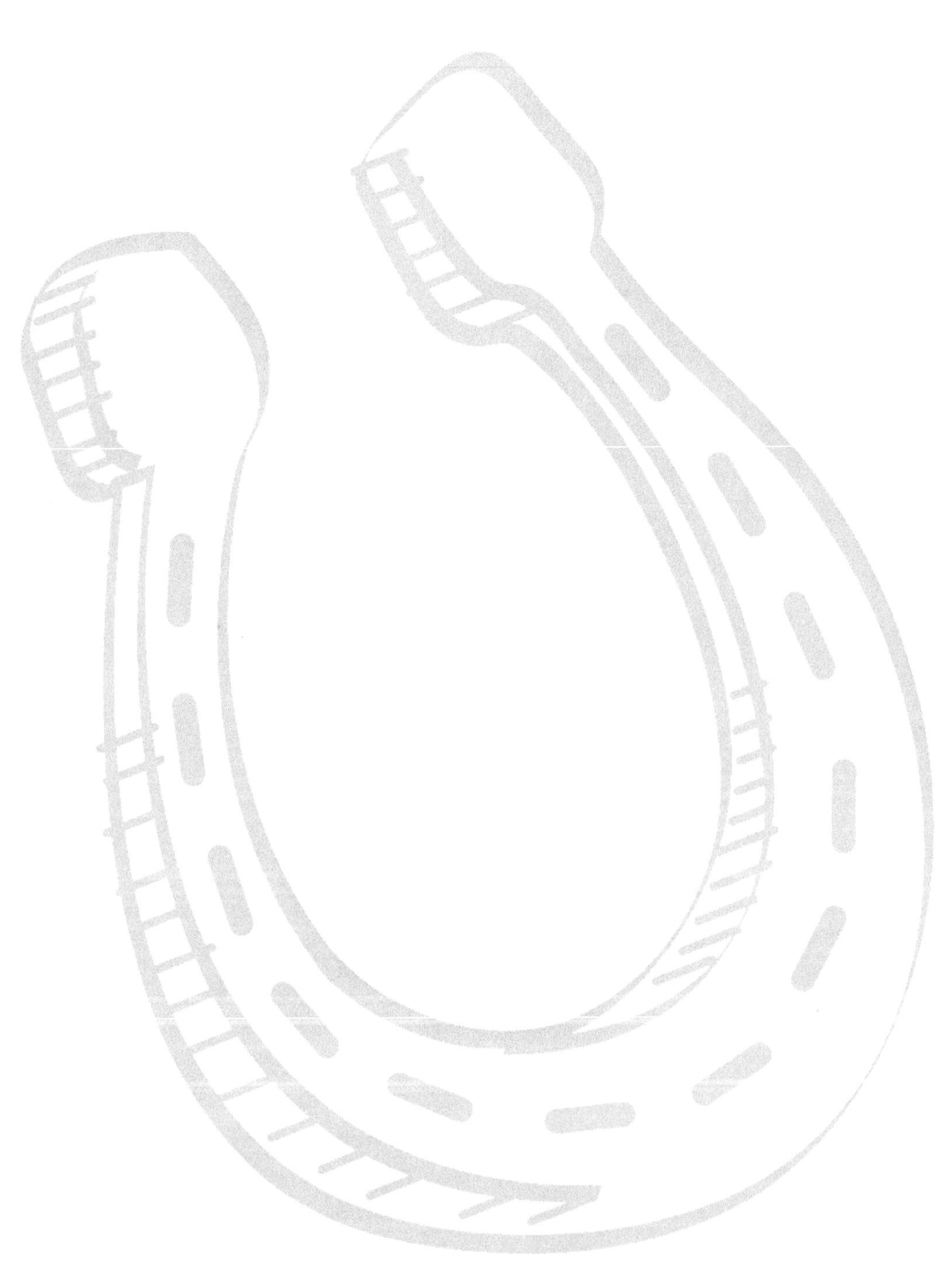

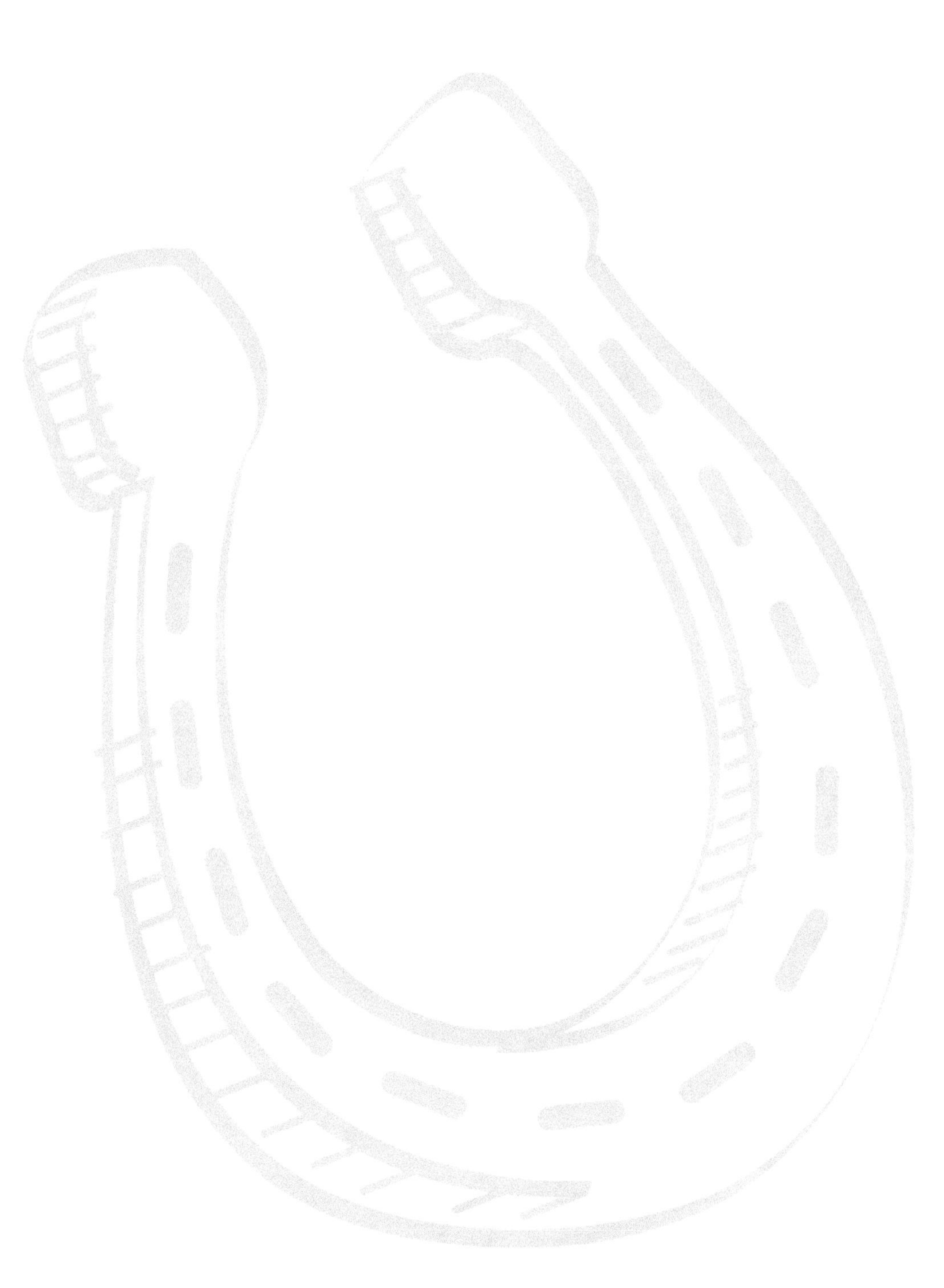

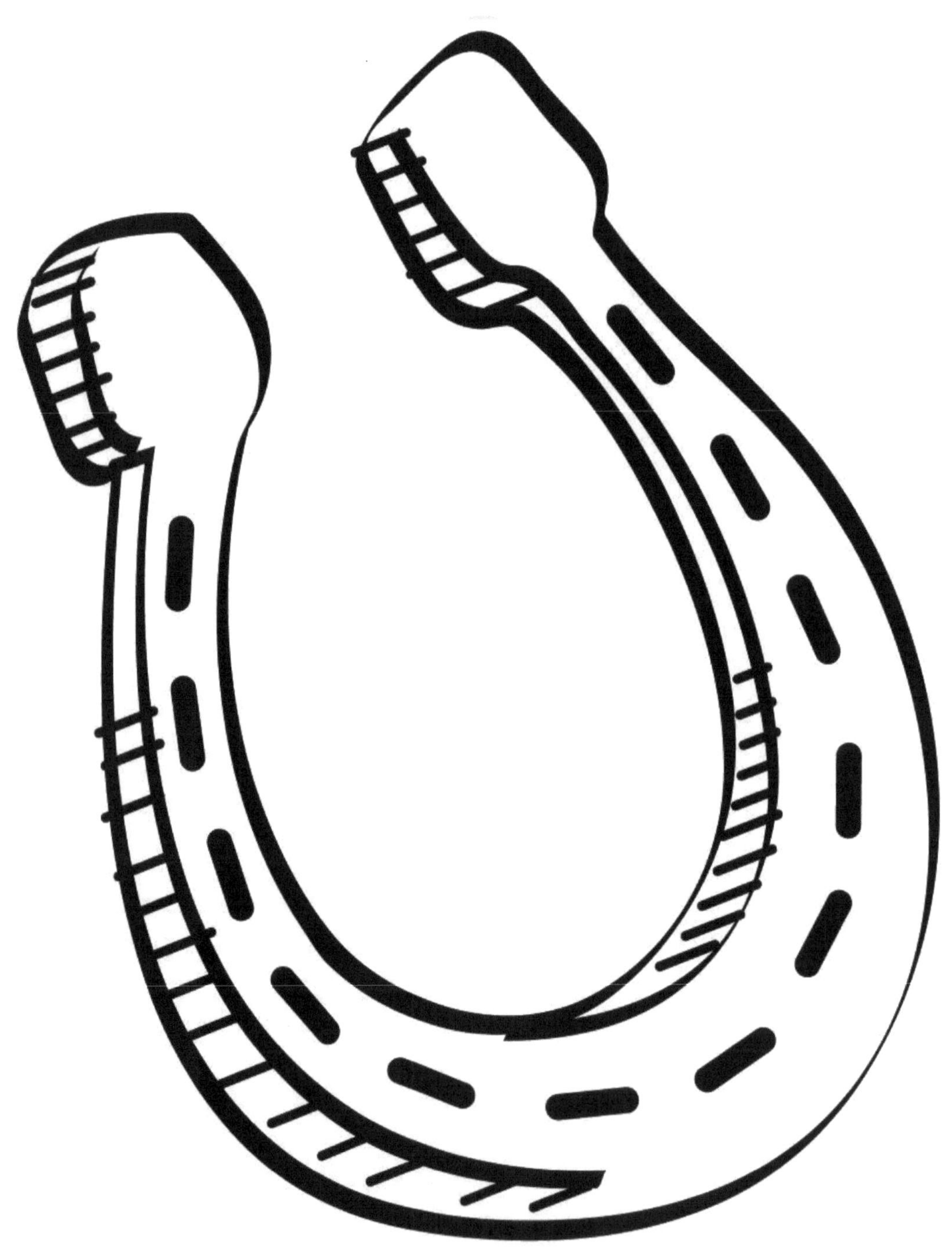

Written & Illustrated by Lori Jahn
© 2015